# The REAL WRITERS' Handbook

TOM ALEXANDER lives in London with his wife and their increasingly irascible cat.

# Contents

Introduction ........................................................................3
Should I use a pen name? ..................................................5
What sort of autograph should I use? ..............................6
How do I know if I'm writing the right thing? ...............7
Who should I dedicate my book to when I finish it?......8
Should I write in the morning or in the evening?..........9
How do I know if I've got the right kind of desk?..........10
What kind of chair should I sit in? ..................................11
What kind of notebook should I have? .............................12
Should I use a laptop or desktop computer? ...................13
Mac or PC? What about Linux? .........................................14
Should I be using specialist writing software? ...............15
Which font should I use? ...................................................16
Should I use a typewriter? ................................................17
Should I write longhand? ..................................................18
What sort of pen should I use? .........................................19
What colour ink should I write in? ..................................20
Should I write in pencil? ...................................................21
What kind of note-taking system should I use? .............22
Where should I write? ........................................................23
Should I write every day? ..................................................24
Should I have a special writing jacket? ...........................25
Should I smoke cigarettes? ...............................................26
Should I drink coffee? ........................................................27
How much alcohol should I drink? ..................................28
Should I take drugs? ..........................................................29

Do I need to wear glasses? ........................................ 30
What sort of music should I listen to? .................... 31
Should I have a blog? ................................................ 32
Should I be on social media? ................................... 33
What sort of friends should I have? ....................... 34
Should I have a pet? .................................................. 35
What kind of shoes should I wear? ........................ 36
What sort of car should I drive? ............................. 37
What should I eat? ..................................................... 38
How much sex should I be having? ........................ 39
What sort of partner should I have? ...................... 40
Should I have an affair? ............................................ 41
Should I be rich or poor? .......................................... 42
What sort of background should I come from? ..... 43
How jealous should I be? .......................................... 44
Should I tell people I'm a writer? ........................... 45
Do I need to be multi-talented? .............................. 46
If writing is my passion, why do I hate it so much? ..... 47
How many books about writing should I have? ..... 48
What if I never make it? ........................................... 49
Conclusion .................................................................. 51

# Introduction

I'm a REAL WRITER.

I know this because I spend a lot of time thinking about what a REAL WRITER I am.

I'm a REAL WRITER because I spend hours that could be spent writing researching software that will make me more productive.

I'm a REAL WRITER because I need a £1000 computer to do the same job as a £250 one.

I'm a REAL WRITER (and everyone knows it) because I sit in coffee shops, wearing my REAL WRITER'S jacket, staring into space and occasionally using my REAL WRITER'S pen to scribble on the pages of my REAL WRITER'S notebook.

I'm a REAL WRITER.

I must be.

Otherwise all the effort spent on these externalities would be a complete waste of time.

Or perhaps not.

Let's be clear: I am not qualified to tell anyone how to write. I don't have the experience, skill or credentials for that. But when it comes to distractions – all the stupid stuff that lives to the side of actually writing – I could teach a masterclass.

That's what this book is. It's all that rubbish, expanded on for just enough time for it to sound plausible and then exposed for the nonsense it is.

Any sensible person wouldn't need a book to spell this out, but what sort of sensible person spends hours sitting by themselves, making things up? Besides, if you're anything like me then you probably you need a message hammered home over and over again before it sinks in.

So, let's get started.

# Should I use a pen name?

I haven't finished the book I'm working on, but I've been thinking about what it will be like when it's published. I don't know whether to publish it under my own name, or use a pseudonym. I think what I'm writing is great, but what if people read it and think it's rubbish? If it's got my own name on it, they might laugh at me. On the other hand, what if they love it, but think that someone else wrote it? I'm getting towards the end of the writing process, but more and more of my attention is caught up on this issue and the book is stalling. I can't go any further until I know the truth: do REAL WRITERS use pen names?

**It doesn't matter. Just write.**

# What sort of autograph should I use?

I haven't had a book signing yet, but am wondering what sort of signature I should use. I've seen some authors use a stylised scrawl on the flyleaf and it makes sense that you'd use something quick and easy if you're signing hundreds of copies. Honestly, though, the fact I couldn't read their name left me feeling a bit short-changed. Is it risky to use your normal signature for your autograph? Does it mean anyone who owns a signed copy could then sign a mortgage application in my name? What sort of autograph do REAL WRITERS use?

**It doesn't matter. Just write.**

# How do I know if I'm writing the right thing?

I'm halfway through writing a pretty long piece of work and it's not going well. I was going great guns in the early stages, but now it's starting to drag. I'm starting to think that maybe it was a mistake to embark on this project and I have an idea for another piece of work that I think will be much better than what I'm working on now. I'm aware, though, that this might just be a form of procrastination. How do REAL WRITERS know if they're writing the right thing?

**It doesn't matter. Just write.**

# Who should I dedicate my book to when I finish it?

I'm in the early stages of a novel and am wondering who I should dedicate it to. I admit that this a long way off, but there are lots of people in my life who have supported my writing. How do I choose which one to dedicate the book to? If I dedicate this one to someone and then it doesn't get published, do I have to dedicate the next one to them as well? What's the system here? How do REAL WRITERS dedicate their books?

**It doesn't matter. Just write.**

# Should I write in the morning or in the evening?

I tend to do my writing late at night, as I like the quiet and still atmosphere. I've read that a lot of authors write first thing in the morning, which makes me think that maybe I'm doing it all wrong. I've always been a night owl and it takes me a long time to get going when I wake up, but maybe I could train myself to get up at the crack of dawn. When do REAL WRITERS do their work?

**It doesn't matter. Just write.**

# How do I know if I've got the right kind of desk?

I usually work at the same desk when I'm writing and I used to love it. Everything was exactly right for how I sat and the way I worked. As a result, I got a lot of writing done. Over time, I find myself getting increasingly uncomfortable while at my desk. My attention wanders, I struggle to find the right position and work doesn't come as easily as it used to. I'm starting to think it's the desk's fault that I don't want to sit at it. Perhaps it's time for an upgrade. What sort of desk do REAL WRITERS use?

**It doesn't matter. Just write.**

# What kind of chair should I sit in?

I've been sitting at my kitchen table to write, using the chairs that came with it. I've been wondering if I should have a special writing chair to use when working. I don't know what that would be exactly – maybe something that swivels around and has fancy arm rests. I just think my writing would be better if I had a proper seat to sit on while I compose my work. What sort of chair do REAL WRITERS sit on?

**It doesn't matter. Just write.**

# What kind of notebook should I have?

I like to take notes by hand, jotting down ideas for scenes and character sketches when they come to me. Usually I use any old piece of paper that's around, but sometimes I lose those pages, so I need a proper notebook. The problem is that there are so many choices! Hardback, softback, big, small, plain, lined, dotted... I don't know where to begin. I've seen people use those Moleskine notebooks but they seem quite expensive when compared to the ones I can get at the supermarket. What sort of notebooks do REAL WRITERS use?

**It doesn't matter. Just write.**

# Should I use a laptop or desktop computer?

I'm stuck in a bit of a quandary in that I don't know what sort of computer I should use for my writing. Previously, I've always used desktop computers because they offer more value for money and I can upgrade the components when I want. I see a lot of people using laptops, though, and I wonder if perhaps my writing would be better if I used a portable computer. I do like working at my usual desk, but maybe I would be better off if I could take my computer with me everywhere. What kind of computers do REAL WRITERS use?

**It doesn't matter. Just write.**

# Mac or PC? What about Linux?

I have a computer that works well enough for my needs, but I wonder if it's projecting the right sort of image. I've always been led to believe that Macs were for creative people, which is why they were more expensive. On the other hand, Windows machines give over the impression of being focussed on work and productivity, without all the faff or frills of the Apple machines. But does it mean I'm not creative if I use a PC? There's also Linux, which seems very complicated and technical, but would show people how clever I am. What operating system does a REAL WRITER use?

**It doesn't matter. Just write.**

# Should I be using specialist writing software?

I've always used the word processor that came with my computer, but I'm seeing all these specialist software packages for writing and I'm wondering if maybe I should use one of those. They offer all sorts of bells and whistles I didn't know I needed, like character sheets, plot timelines and special export functions. The program I currently use doesn't do much apart from let me put words on the page. What sort of software do REAL WRITERS use?

**It doesn't matter. Just write.**

# Which font should I use?

My understanding is that publishers and agents usually prefer manuscripts submitted in Times New Roman or something similar, but what's the best font for actually working on a manuscript? I find my eyes gloss over Times a bit, but some of these specialist writing apps use monospaced fonts like Menlo. Is it really so bad to use a serif font like Helvetica or Arial? What's the font of choice for a REAL WRITER?

**It doesn't matter. Just write.**

# Should I use a typewriter?

I know that everyone uses computers these days, but part of me really yearns for the mechanical clackity-clack of an old-fashioned typewriter. I realise it's inconvenient, but when I think of all those great novels written on a typewriter, I can't help but think there's some kind of mojo in those machines. Would getting a typewriter make me a REAL WRITER?

**It doesn't matter. Just write.**

# Should I write longhand?

I usually work on the computer as I find it's quicker and I get into a better flow. I read somewhere that Hemingway said everyone should write their first drafts by hand as it forces them to rewrite when they have to type it up. I've also heard other writers say that writing by hand slows them down, forcing them to consider every word. But then, there's other people who say they only work on a keyboard. It's so confusing. Do REAL WRITERS work longhand?

**It doesn't matter. Just write.**

# What sort of pen should I use?

When I write by hand, I usually grab whatever pen is closest. I have a couple of brands that I like, but they're pretty cheap and I wonder if I would be a better writer if I invested in an expensive fountain pen. I've never got on with them in the past, as I find that the ink smudges and I make a mess. Still, I could learn to live with it if I had to. What sort of pen do REAL WRITERS use?

**It doesn't matter. Just write.**

# What colour ink should I write in?

I used to be a die-hard black ink user, believing that blue should only be used by secretaries and editors. The other day, however, I used a blue pen to draft longhand and I really liked the way it looked – less austere and confrontational than black ink, which now seems really stark. I kind of want to use blue ink more regularly but worry that it's betraying my principles as a black ink user. What's more, I'm hearing that some authors use other colours in their pens like brown or green! I'm so confused. Tell me, what colour do REAL WRITERS write in?

**It doesn't matter. Just write.**

# Should I write in pencil?

I went to the stationers the other day and found some very expensive pencils. I was a little taken aback at the price (along with the cost of a special sharpener) but the person behind the counter said they were the type of pencils used by famous authors in the 20<sup>th</sup> century. I suppose the good thing about pencils is you can rub out your mistakes, but I don't know if I should spend all that money on them or not. Do REAL WRITERS use pencils?

**It doesn't matter. Just write.**

# What kind of note-taking system should I use?

I like to take notes about projects I'm working on or may write in the future. Usually, I put these in a notebook for me to come back to later, but I've seen all sorts of people saying I should be using note-taking software that relies on folders, tags and workflows. It all seems a bit complicated to me, but I don't want to be left behind. What sort of note-taking system do REAL WRITERS use?

**It doesn't matter. Just write.**

# Where should I write?

Usually I write at home, but I often see people working in coffee shops. I have a laptop, so I could go to one, but there's always music playing and chatter in the background, which I find distracting. I've tried going to the library, thinking it would be quieter, but there's usually someone watching YouTube videos without wearing headphones. Where do REAL WRITERS do their work?

**It doesn't matter. Just write.**

# Should I write every day?

I have quite a busy life and have to fit in my writing around other responsibilities like work, family and my social life. For the most part, I'm pretty happy with this balance, but I've read things saying that you must write every single day and that if you don't, you're not taking your writing seriously. I think I'm doing OK, but do you have to write every day to be a REAL WRITER?

**It doesn't matter. Just write.**

# Should I have a special writing jacket?

I don't have much of a routine when it comes to writing – I just do it when I get the chance. That said, I'm starting to wonder if perhaps I should start dressing the part. I've often seen writers in photographs wearing suit jackets and I wonder if wearing one helps the process. What sort of jackets do REAL WRITERS wear?

**It doesn't matter. Just write.**

# Should I smoke cigarettes?

When I look at the great authors from the past, I can't help but notice that a lot of them smoked cigarettes. I know all about the health risks and the costs involved in the habit, but I also think it looks kind of cool and I wonder if maybe smoking is the missing ingredient in my working practice. Whether it's pen in one hand, cigarette in the other, or having a lit one dangling from my lips at I pound away at the keyboard, I can't help but feel it would enhance my productivity. So, tell the truth – do REAL WRITERS smoke?

**It doesn't matter. Just write.**

# Should I drink coffee?

I get the impression that that a lot of authors drink bucketloads of coffee. I don't really like the taste, it makes me jittery and I find I have to go to the loo a lot. That said, if it makes my writing better then I suppose I could learn to like it. Do REAL WRITERS drink coffee?

**It doesn't matter. Just write.**

# How much alcohol should I drink?

I've never really been much of a drinker. I might have a glass of wine with dinner or maybe a cold beer on a summer day. You hear so much about the drinking exploits of famous authors and literary memoirs are full of boozy benders and drunken scrapes. If I want to be taken seriously, do I need to become an alcoholic? How much do REAL WRITERS drink?

**It doesn't matter. Just write.**

# Should I take drugs?

Some of my favourite authors are known for their experimentation with drugs and I'm wondering if this is something that I should explore. It seems to me that there are untapped parts of my mind that can only be accessed with narcotics. Legality aside, I wonder if perhaps taking loads of drugs would make my work better. Do I need to take drugs in order to be a REAL WRITER?

**It doesn't matter. Just write.**

# Do I need to wear glasses?

I have 20/20 vision, but always like the look of spectacles. It hasn't escaped my attention that a lot of writers wear them and obviously it gives them a kind of intellectual aura that I wouldn't mind cultivating myself. I'm considering getting some clear-lensed glasses or maybe doing something to my eyes that would necessitate prescription lenses. Do I need to wear glasses to consider myself a REAL WRITER?

**It doesn't matter. Just write.**

# What sort of music should I listen to?

I sometimes have music playing in the background while I'm writing, but I'm wondering whether I'm listening to the right things for my writing career. I've seen interviews with authors where they say they can't listen to music with lyrics, because it interferes with their word choices. Others say they're inspired by classical music or complex jazz, but that's not really my cup of tea. What sort of music do REAL WRITERS listen to?

It doesn't matter. Just write.

# Should I have a blog?

I know that blogs are having a bit of a resurgence at the moment, so I was wondering whether I should start one. I'm not really sure what I would write about, but maybe it would be good exercise. On the other hand, perhaps it would be a distraction from my other writing and I have enough of those already. My concern is that I won't be taken seriously if I don't have one. Do REAL WRITERS have to have blogs?

**It doesn't matter. Just write.**

# Should I be on social media?

Like everyone these days, I have accounts to various social media sites. Some are for staying in touch with friends and family, others are for viewing funny or interesting things. I keep hearing that authors should use social media to grow their audience, but I don't know how to do that, or if I even want to. Can I be a REAL WRITER if I'm not a social media influencer?

**It doesn't matter. Just write.**

# What sort of friends should I have?

I'm lucky in that I have some really good friends who have been with me through thick and thin. But now that I'm thinking seriously about my writing, I'm wondering if they fit in to the version of myself I want to create. Most of my friends have regular jobs and I'm wondering whether I should ditch them and surround myself with creative types and quirky characters that can serve as fodder for my writing. What sort of friends do REAL WRITERS have?

**It doesn't matter. Just write.**

# Should I have a pet?

Sometimes I see photographs of authors at home and they often have a dog by their side or a cat at their feet. Is having a pet a job requirement for being a writer? I could get one, but if the marketplace is already crowded with cats and dogs, maybe I would be better off with something a little more unusual, like a parrot or a gecko. Or would that be pretentious? Do REAL WRITERS have pets?

**It doesn't matter. Just write.**

# What kind of shoes should I wear?

I usually wear comfortable shoes like trainers, but I wonder if people don't take my writing seriously because of them. Is there a type of shoe I should be wearing that would make my writing seem more authentic? Or is there any type of footwear I should particularly avoid? What do REAL WRITERS wear on their feet?

**It doesn't matter. Just write.**

# What sort of car should I drive?

I once saw a well-known novelist do an illegal u-turn in a Nissan Micra. I was under the impression that published authors drove expensive BMWs or lovingly restored classic cars, but maybe I should be driving a crappy hatchback? Perhaps it would be better not to have a car at all and use public transport, as that would allow me time to write on the train or the bus. What mode of transport do REAL WRITERS use?

**It doesn't matter. Just write.**

# What should I eat?

I have always had a fairly balanced diet, but now that I'm a writer, I wonder if perhaps I need to look at what I'm consuming and how it affects my work. There's all sorts of information on the internet about eating to maximise brain efficiency. Should I start learning about that? Conversely, it seems like some authors have terrible diets, eating really unhealthy food. It's so confusing. What do REAL WRITERS eat?

**It doesn't matter. Just write.**

# How much sex should I be having?

Whenever I read literary memoirs, it seems that there's an awful lot of sex in them. I've always thought I had a fairly normal sex drive, but it seems like if you want to be considered a really great author, you either need to be shagging loads or have a crippling dysfunction in the bedroom. I don't think I've got the temperament for either, but I suppose I could learn. How much sex do REAL WRITERS have?

**It doesn't matter. Just write.**

# What sort of partner should I have?

I love my partner very much, but I'm not sure they're a "writer's partner", if you know what I mean. They're very nice and I'm still attracted to them, but I wonder if my writing might be better if I was with someone else. I think about the passionate relationships of writers such as Scott and Zelda Fitzgerald and wonder if maybe alcoholism and insanity would kick my writing up a notch. What kind of spouse would make me a REAL WRITER?

**It doesn't matter. Just write.**

# Should I have an affair?

It seems like all my literary idols were having extra-marital affairs and it's made me wonder if I should be doing the same. There are so many novels written about infidelity that it seems to be one of the enduring themes of not only great literature, but also great writers. If I'm in a monogamous relationship, would cheating on my partner make my writing better? Or, if single, should I seek out a married person to sleep with? Does having an affair make me a REAL WRITER?

**It doesn't matter. Just write.**

# Should I be rich or poor?

I know that writing is rarely a big-money profession, but is that part of the lustre? I've been wondering lately whether being poor is better for writing, as it gives you grit and determination to pull yourself up by the bootstraps. Or is it better not to have to worry about how to pay for the roof over your head and just be able to concentrate on the work? If you want to be a REAL WRITER, is it better to be rich or poor?

**It doesn't matter. Just write.**

## What sort of background should I come from?

None of my family are in the creative industries, all having what you would probably call 'normal jobs'. I don't know whether this is a detriment to my writing career. I have no experience of being a creative professional and think that perhaps it would be better to have this from the jump. If my parents were artists and my siblings were composers and film producers, would that make me a REAL WRITER?

**It doesn't matter. Just write.**

## How jealous should I be?

Through my writing, I've got to know a few other authors and we keep abreast of each other's careers. Lately, some of them have become more successful than me and while I'm pleased for them, I do feel a bit jealous of their accomplishments. I wonder, though, whether this envy might not be a good thing. I often hear of literary rivals, spurring each other on to greater heights. Should I be cultivating this envy as a source of fuel? How jealous should a REAL WRITER be?

**It doesn't matter. Just write.**

## Should I tell people I'm a writer?

I've been writing for a while now and I've had some successes, but nothing too major. I feel like I'm making progress in my writing., but I don't know if I've earned the right to call myself a writer, given that it's not my main source of income. Do REAL WRITERS tell people they're writers, or keep it to themselves?

It doesn't matter. Just write.

# Do I need to be multi-talented?

Writing has always been my creative outlet, but it seems there are some authors who seem to be equally talented in other areas. I see them painting or playing music and I wonder if maybe I should be using my writing time doing other creative endeavours. I think it would be nice to be a polymath, but I've never really been very good at anything else. Do I have to be good at other things to be a REAL WRITER?

**It doesn't matter. Just write.**

## If writing is my passion, why do I hate it so much?

I've been writing, or trying to write, for a long time now. People know me as a writer and it often comes up in conversation. When I tell them I'm sick of it and I want to give up, they tell me that I can't do that and they call it 'my passion'. The only thing passionate about it is how much I hate it, but I can't seem to stop. If I hate writing, am I a REAL WRITER?

**It doesn't matter. Just write.**

# How many books about writing should I have?

Obviously I like to read, but I find books about writing to be a bit of a bore. I want to hone my craft and I know that I have a lot still to learn, but when I've finished on my own work I just want to put my feet up and dive into somebody else's world for a while. Do you have to read books about writing to be a REAL WRITER?

**It doesn't matter. Just write.**

# What if I never make it?

I've been writing for some time now and it feels like I'm getting nowhere. I send off manuscripts, outlines and proposals and most of the time I don't hear anything back – not even a 'no'. Writing has never been my main source of income and now it's looking like it never will be. I still enjoy the work and can't imagine giving it up, but I'm wondering if perhaps it might not be my career and this is a source of shame for me. If I don't make money from my work, can I still be a REAL WRITER?

**It doesn't matter. Just write.**

# What if I never make it?

It doesn't matter, just write.

# Conclusion

The idea that there's someone out there, doing it perfectly, with all the right stuff and in all the right ways, is nonsense.

Everybody struggles.

Everyone gets distracted.

We all lose heart sometimes.

There is no perfect pen, no notebook that unlocks talent and no lifestyle choice that will make everything fall into place.

All there is – all there has ever been – is the work itself.

Writing.

And if you're doing that, you are a REAL WRITER.

*Also available*

**FORMS**
by Tom Alexander

The book of fun paperwork for you to fill in at your leisure. Contains 30 original pieces of admin (black biro not included).

Available on Amazon, tomalexander.org or order it from your local bookshop.